The Miller Garden: Icon of Mode

By Gary R. Hilderbrand

Introduction by David Dillon

Photography by Ezra Stoller and Alan Ward

S P A C E M A K E R   P R E S S

Washington, DC

Cambridge, MA

Acknowledgments

Front cover: The Honeylocust Allée,
photograph by Alan Ward.
Pages 28, 29, 32, 34 by Gary R. Hilderbrand.
Page 27 courtesy of The Frances Loeb Library,
Graduate School of Design, Harvard University.
Drawings: © Dan Kiley, courtesy of
The Frances Loeb Library, Graduate School
of Design, Harvard University.

Publisher: James G. Trulove
Editor and Art Director: Sarah Vance
Designer: Elizabeth Reifeiss
Printer: Palace Press International
ISBN: 1-888931-07-8
Copyright © 1999
Spacemaker Press®
All rights reserved.

The Miller Garden: Icon of Modernism
was first prepared under the title "In
the Light of the Miller Garden" for a
symposium on the early work of Dan
Kiley, sponsored in November 1997
by the Graduate School of Design,
Harvard University. I am grateful to
Irwin and Xenia Miller for permission
to visit the garden on several occasions, and to Jim Shearn, the grounds
supervisor, for his generous time and
his insights. Also, thanks to Allyson
Mendenhall for research assistance,
and Mary Daniels, Jane Amidon, and
Peter Papademetriou for archival
support. I am grateful to Alan Ward for
his inspired work, and to David Dillon,
Sarah Vance, Melanie Simo, and
Douglas Reed for their helpful
comments. Dan Donovan has shared
with me his insights and interpreta-
tions of Kiley's work at Hollin Hills.
Thanks, finally, to Dan Kiley.

Contents

Portfolio: Photographs by Ezra Stoller 1958

Ezra Stoller, the leading photographer of modern architecture in America for decades, photographed the Miller House for Eero Saarinen in 1958. Several of his images appeared in "A Contemporary Palladian Villa," in *The Architectural Forum*, in 1958. Some of those are included here, along with several images never before published.

This is a rare view of the drive and house,
showing Kiley's Horsechestnut trees in
relation to the Arborvitae hedge.

Space for cars dominates the
principal facade. The main entrance
to the house is just beyond.

The view through the central space of the house, framed by the Honeylocust allée, extends to the meadow and the Flatrock River beyond.

The podium and roof define a space of transparency between inside and outside.

*Paired Magnolias give spatial definition to
the podium on the north side of the house.*

The house and its surrounding spaces sit gracefully above the meadow, on the floodplain's natural levee.

A Place No One Knows

by David Dillon

Visitors to Columbus, Indiana, can pick up a pocket map at the chamber of commerce and in a matter of hours get a short course in modern American architecture. With churches by Eliel and Eero Saarinen, a fire station from Robert Venturi, schools by Harry Weese, Richard Meier, and Edward Larrabee Barnes, the community is dotted with significant buildings by distinguished architects. A Henry Moore sculpture stands in front of I.M. Pei's public library, while a kinetic Jean Tinguely construction anchors a downtown shopping mall designed by Cesar Pelli. For a small prairie town known for corn and diesel engines, Columbus (pop. 33,000) makes a remarkably cosmopolitan impression.

But one stop not on any tour is the house and garden belonging to the town's preeminent architectural patron—J. Irwin Miller. Tucked away on a narrow side street among conventionally eclectic Georgian and Tudor mansions, the Miller House is discretion itself. No porte-cochere or grand ceremonial entrance. Not even

an identifiable front door. Instead of imperiously straddling the driveway, it stands quietly to one side—more edge than object.

Designed between 1953 and 1957 by Eero Saarinen and Kevin Roche, the Miller House is a refined period piece of the same vintage as Mies van der Rohe's Farnsworth House and the Glass House by Philip Johnson—clear, transparent, structurally expressive objects in luxuriant natural settings.

But the Miller Garden, designed by Dan Kiley, seems outside of time, a modernist icon that is as fresh and provocative today as when it was new. Every contemporary landscape architect has read about it, heard about it, seen photographs of it. Yet few have actually set foot in it. The reasons for this paradox range from Columbus's geographical isolation—50 miles south of Indianapolis—to the Millers' insistence on privacy. As the wealthy parents of five young children, they were understandably concerned about security. And as native Hoosiers, they were constitutionally incapable of display and self-promotion. To others they may have been Columbus's first family, but in their own eyes they were "just folks." No Columbus building bears the Miller name; nor does it appear on Irwin Miller's office door or his stationery. For decades, requests to visit and photograph the house were politely denied, sometimes with an apologetic note from Mrs. Miller explaining the family's uneasiness about publicity. On the few occasions when the house did show up in print it was identified only as "a residence in the Midwest," with no mention of the owner or the location.[1]

With their children grown and gone, the Millers have become more accommodating. The garden has appeared in several recent landscape histories, and the 1994 Pritzker Prize dinner was served in Dan Kiley's celebrated Honeylocust allée, with its sweeping views of the meadows and the Flatrock River. Yet in spite of its iconic status, the Miller Garden remains surprisingly elusive and enigmatic, like a tantalizing rumor that can't be pinned down.

Main entrance to the house

13

The Miller House in Context

The Miller House and Garden evolved from a three-cornered collaboration among architects Eero Saarinen, Kevin Roche, and Alexander Girard, landscape architect Dan Kiley, and owners J. Irwin and Xenia Miller.

The Miller-Saarinen association began in the 1930s when Irwin Miller returned home from Yale and Oxford to manage Cummins Engine Company, a family business that had been losing money for 15 years. Only 24 and extremely scholarly—he read Plato and Cicero in the original and played Bach on his Stradivarius—Miller saw immediately that Cummins couldn't survive selling only to other engine makers. It had to persuade struggling truckers that they'd make more money by specifying Cummins engines. This "back door" strategy paid off. Within three years Cummins was in the black and on its way to becoming the largest diesel engine manufacturer in the world. And Miller was on his way to becoming a patron of modern architecture.

The Millers belonged to the First Christian Church—Irwin Miller's maternal grandfather had been its most celebrated preacher—and when the time came to build a new sanctuary the family donated the land and half the construction costs. At Miller's prompting, they also chose the architect—Eliel Saarinen.

Saarinen was a bold choice for a conservative community accustomed to ranch houses and traditional Victorian storefronts. Runner-up in the 1922 Chicago Tribune Tower Competition, then designer and director of the influential Cranbrook Academy of Art near Detroit, Saarinen was a link between the Arts and Crafts movement of the late 19th century and the first surge of modernism in the early 20th century.

Completed in 1942, the First Christian Church remains one of Columbus's finest buildings, a blend of graceful proportions, handsome craft details—bannisters, moldings, light fixtures—and spare modern volumes. On the flat prairie landscape it is an instant landmark, its soaring bell tower anchoring the downtown like a campanile in an Italian piazza. The surrounding gardens, which originally spread beneath the school and administrative wing, reach out toward the old city hall and the new county library, integrating the ecclesiastical and civic landscapes. In his concern for creating total environments, Eliel Saarinen set an important example for his son Eero.

Eero occasionally accompanied Eliel to Columbus, and while his father met with the church building committee, he and Irwin Miller would stroll downtown for lunch and conversation. They shared a passion for modern architecture and an unshakable faith in new technology. They maintained their friendship through the war by means of letters and occasional dinners in Washington, where Eero was head of the Special Exhibits Section of the Office of Strategic Services (OSS), the military precursor of the CIA. The exhibits section prepared elaborate maps and charts for the Pentagon on shipping routes, bombing targets, and other military intelligence. It was an ideal job for an architect. And when Eero departed in early 1945 he chose Dan Kiley as his successor. Kiley later parlayed the job into a commission to design the courtroom for the Nuremberg trials.

Eliel Saarinen died in 1950 and Eero took over the practice. Shortly thereafter Irwin Miller hired him and Alexander Girard, a consultant on the Saarinens's vast General Motors Technical Center in Warren, Michigan, to design their lake house in Muskoka, Ontario, north of Toronto.

Miller brought Eero back in 1953 to design the Irwin Union Bank and Trust in downtown Columbus. A flat-roofed, steel and glass pavilion, it introduced the International Style to Main Street. Dan Kiley surrounded the base with thick ground cover and placed the drive-up windows in a grove of trees to connect inside and outside. "We wanted a bank that was transparent, that would let people see what we were doing with their money," Irwin Miller later explained. "We wanted to take the mystery out of banking."[2]

But he wanted more than that; he wanted to put Columbus on the map. Coming from a family of preachers, he knew all the appropriate texts on good works and individual responsibility for the common welfare. And as an ardent modernist he believed that architecture was one way to do both. In 1954, he established the Cummins Engine Foundation, which agreed to pay the design fees on new public buildings provided the architects were chosen from an approved list. The first lists were put together by Miller, Saarinen, and architect Pietro Belluschi. Predictably many of the early commissions went to members of the Saarinen circle: Gunnar Birkerts, Paul Kennon, Cesar Pelli, Harry Weese, and Robert Venturi. As the program developed the work was more evenly distributed between established practitioners and rising young stars, such as Emilio Ambasz, Taft Architects, and landscape architect Michael Van Valkenburgh. A job in Columbus, even a small one, is still a coveted imprimatur.

Miller's initial objective was to raise the design standards of public schools in Columbus, which had plummeted during the postwar construction boom. Within a decade the program had expanded to include libraries, fire stations, parks, recreation centers, and golf courses. To date, the Cummins Engine Foundation has funded at least 50 public projects, and subtly influenced numerous private ones, including churches, private homes, even the printing plant of Columbus's daily newspaper, The Republic.

"The future of Columbus depends on the attitudes of its people," Miller said in the 1960s. "The impact of these buildings on them is very subtle; it may take 100 years to show."[3] It showed much sooner. Modern architecture has turned out to be Columbus's best advertisement, attracting nearly 200,000 visitors annually and enabling Cummins and other local companies to recruit bright young managers and engineers who might never have given a small, Mid-American town a second thought. It has given the place an identity, made it memorable and more livable.

The Evolution of the Miller House

Irwin and Xenia Miller wanted their new home to be progressive yet unpretentious—like themselves. In the early 1950s they had purchased a sloping 10-acre site on the edge of town, overlooking the Flatrock River. Its remoteness satisfied their desire for privacy, while its general openness—corn had once grown on the bluff, tobacco in the bottomland—provided a *tabula rasa* on which to conduct an experiment in modern living. The only givens were a few large trees on the perimeter of the site, and a floodplain at the bottom.

Once again the Millers turned to the triumvirate of Saarinen, Roche, and Girard for the basic architectural design. As soon as the house was under construction Saarinen brought in Dan Kiley, his successor at OSS and later his associate on both the master plan for Antioch College in Ohio and the "Gateway Arch" competition in St. Louis.

The Millers' program was brief and basic: privacy without walling out the neighbors; a concealed private entrance; color in the spring and fall, when they were in residence; a design that fit the place, and that differed from both their lake house in Canada and their nondescript ranch house in Columbus.

"I don't know that we ever used the words modern or contemporary," says Irwin Miller, "but we wanted the house to grow out of Columbus, which is flat and on a grid. A curvy design on this landscape wouldn't have looked right."[4]

Discussions went on for nearly two years, with the architects proposing and the Millers politely disposing of half a dozen schemes.

One located the house on a sand bar in the river, with three sides surrounded by earthen "berms" and only one open to the landscape. It was quickly dropped as unbuildable.

A later, more minimalist design showed a house on stilts in the river flood plain. It also got only one look. "We told Eero we didn't want to live in a tree house," recalls Mrs. Miller.

A third proposal called for the house to be partially sunken into the slope, following the same basic plan as the house that was finally built except for smaller windows. The Millers found it too gloomy.

"We never told Eero or Kevin what to do," says Xenia Miller, "but we always felt free to send them back to the drawing board if there was something we didn't like."

Saarinen went back so often that finally he insisted on a new contract. "He told us we were too expensive to work for on a percentage basis," recalls Irwin Miller. "So he started charging us by the hour. That way, he said, we could talk as long as we wanted."

The final plan is a modified nine-square grid, with the central bay slightly wider than the others to energize the composition and set it in motion. The house sits on a low podium, its private spaces pushed to the four corners and the more public ones—living room, dining room—grouped around a "conversation pit" in the middle. The similarities to the centralized plans of renaissance villas are obvious, but the house's low projecting roof, floating above

The common spaces—entry, living room, and dining room—grouped around a "conversation pit"

large planes of glass, belongs unmistakably to the 1950s, when Mies, Philip Johnson, Craig Ellwood and other modernists made it the all purpose solution to the problem of connecting indoor and outdoor spaces.

According to project architect Kevin Roche, the idea of the glass walls came from Girard, who had designed his own house in Grosse Pointe, Michigan, with two garage doors that could be raised to connect inside and outside. The house also featured a sunken conversation pit that became the prototype for the Millers.

Girard, a slight, energetic man in his mid-forties, was as intense as Saarinen but also more playful and more comfortable with the small domestic details that make houses livable. He once described himself as "a reasonable and sane functionalist, tempered by irrational frivolity"—a modernist with the soul of a folk artist. He combined fascination with modern technology with a childlike delight in texture, color, and pattern. He could become as absorbed in

drawer pulls or the folds in a drape as in a plan, which made him the perfect person to humanize Saarinen's rigorous and severely intellectualized design.

"He had great sensitivity to the art of living in a house with a family," says Roche. "And he expressed it by bringing all of his stuff along and implanting it. But it was very livable stuff. He made [the Miller House] a home."[5] For "stuff" read furniture, antiques, textiles, and art that Girard and the Millers collected on their shopping expeditions to New York, London, and Central America. Some pieces they acquired from exhibitions that Girard had curated at the Museum of Modern Art, for which he then created new domestic settings. He also designed tables, storage cabinets, rugs (incorporating leaf patterns from trees on the site), even napkin rings for the children, each imprinted with a different design. He later designed the Irwin Management Company offices and renovated several blocks of Victorian buildings in downtown Columbus.

Saarinen was happy to turn over the domestic details to someone else. By the mid-1950s his career was in overdrive, with the GM Tech Center at its peak, the work for MIT and IBM under way, and the TWA Terminal and Dulles Airport on the horizon. The last thing he wanted to worry about was where to hang the bath towels.

Creating the Miller Garden

Eero Saarinen and Dan Kiley likewise made an intriguing team—the one intense, aggressive, consumed by architecture, the other elfin, expansive, and given to benignly subversive behavior that either charmed or exasperated clients.

Dan Kiley and Irwin Miller first met at a luncheon at the Palm Cafe in Columbus in 1955. An abstainer but a gracious host, Miller asked if anyone wanted a cocktail. Dead silence, until Dan piped up to order a double scotch. Another long silence, followed by a ripple of eager hands around the room. "It turned into a pretty good party," Kiley recalls.[7]

Irwin Miller apparently thought so too, because shortly thereafter Kiley and his family were on their way to the Millers' lake house in Muskoka in their Volkswagen bus.

"I'm loose and open and a bit irresponsible," Kiley says. "I think Irwin got a kick out of me, in his Hoosier sort of way."

Although by this time Kiley had designed numerous residential gardens, he was still known primarily for his corporate and institutional work (IBM, Union Carbide, Concordia College) in which he served as planning consultant as well as landscape architect. But when he arrived in Columbus the site plan was complete and the house under construction ("All covered with plywood and looking like an airplane hangar," he remembers) so he was forced to play off what Saarinen had already done.

Kiley says he felt the house was too self-contained to be connected to the landscape linearly by allées and other formal devices.

"It was a house in the round, like Villa Rotonda, so I began thinking about making pinwheeling spaces exploding out into the landscape. The basic idea came very quickly. I don't remember doing more than a few sketches."

Essentially, Kiley created a series of green rooms that extended the centrifugal energy of Saarinen's floor plan to the boundaries of the site. Spaces open, unfold, and overlap as they do within the house, breaking free of their orthogonal straightjacket to become dynamic and surprising. Allées become screens and filters; grids of trees enclose dramatic pools of light at their centers.

"Eero and Kevin never questioned anything I did," says Kiley. "But I also recognized that they had placed this big piece of sculpture in space so I couldn't put big trees around it. Almost everything had to happen away from the building."

Kiley's architectural contribution was to persuade Saarinen to reduce the depth of the house podium from 25 to 10 feet and to use the captured space for ground cover and a few small trees.

As a counterpoint to the formal geometry of the plateau, Kiley later proposed a romantic garden for the lower meadow that included "watercourses and pools of different character [and] walks which reveal statues and banks of flowers and pass through a rich variety of different spaces and sensory experiences."[7]

A picturesque garden is a familiar element in "Palladian" villas in

England and playing soft, picturesque details against crisp classical geometry is a familiar Kiley device. But the Millers would have none of it.

"There was supposed to be a Henry Moore and Rodin's 'The Kiss' was to be in a little pavilion," Kiley explained years later. "Doug Sampson, who worked for me then, drew 'The Kiss' so real that I think it embarrassed the Millers a little and they never built it. It almost embarrassed me."

Kiley calls the Miller Garden his "first truly modern landscape," which is to say one of the first truly modern landscapes in America.

"The Millers were the first clients who gave me the freedom to do a complete geometry on the land," he says. "I could introduce original concepts to them without having to argue. The garden also fit their personalities. It was clear, understandable, orderly, and conservative."

But the Miller Garden didn't just happen. It culminated a series of spatial experiments begun at Hollin Hills, Virginia, several years earlier. As part of their contracts, developer Robert Davenport required homeowners to buy a landscape plan from Dan Kiley for $150. The fee was so low, Kiley recalls, that he had to do three or four a day to make money. Most of the plans were quite conventional, but a few were prophetic and employed the use of features found at the Millers'—grids, allées, hedges, and outdoor rooms.

Of the nearly 100 plans that Kiley produced for Hollin Hills, only a handful were carried out. The big payoff would come in the Miller Garden.

"They were very receptive clients," says Kevin Roche. "Irwin in particular had a penetrating eye that cleared away all the detritus that architects produce, without compromising the design in any way. He disciplined Dan, Eero, and Girard, or created situations in which they disciplined themselves."

Kiley's correspondence with the Millers confirms this impression. No detail was beneath notice. They haunted nurseries, devoured technical manuals, regularly sought advice on cutting and pruning. In one letter they ask Kiley about replacing several Yellowood trees; in another they speculate on the possible effects of soaking spring rains on the young Arborvitae hedges. "They were loyal to it," says Kiley.

Thanks to the Millers' extraordinary stewardship, the garden has retained an almost pre-lapsarian lushness, mature without being old, as though it had magically defied time and change.

In Pursuit of Modern Space:
The Garden Plans for Hollin Hills

Although Dan Kiley describes the Miller Garden as his first modern project, this statement overshadows the spatial experiments and achievements of much of his work in the years before 1955. His many garden plans for Virginia developer Robert Davenport at Hollin Hills, outside Washington, D.C., are an extraordinary example. Kiley proposed designs for nearly one hundred residential plots for Davenport between 1952 and 1955. Few of these were implemented according to Kiley's plans, but the collection of drawings produced by his office for Hollin Hills illustrates a number of the spatial themes that were pursued by Kiley during this period—indeed, they suggest a working search for spatial form that lays the groundwork for Kiley's plan for the Miller Garden of August, 1955.

Davenport's development scheme consisted of simple but spatially engaging wood-frame houses on wooded, sloping lots. House type and orientation varied with the irregular terrain and lot configurations. Kiley produced a single developed plan for each property, always resolving the shape of the site with the position of the house, the configuration of adjacent plots, and the relation to the street. Programmatically, the projects demonstrate a convergence of traditional uses and modern conveniences. With occasional inventiveness, Kiley reconciles the conventional spaces for drying yards, vegetable gardens with dedicated play spaces for children, and modern, efficient terraces related to the interior living spaces. The organization of paved areas, pathways, plantings, and parking often depends on angular or concentric figural shapes that either reflect the lines of the house or contrast with its rectilinear nature. One aspect that points toward the kind of ambition for communal lifestyle that was envisioned here— buyers in Hollin Hills were identified

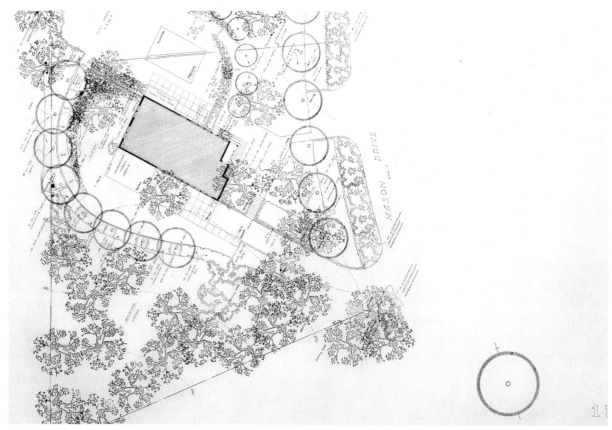

Coffin Residence July 2, 1954

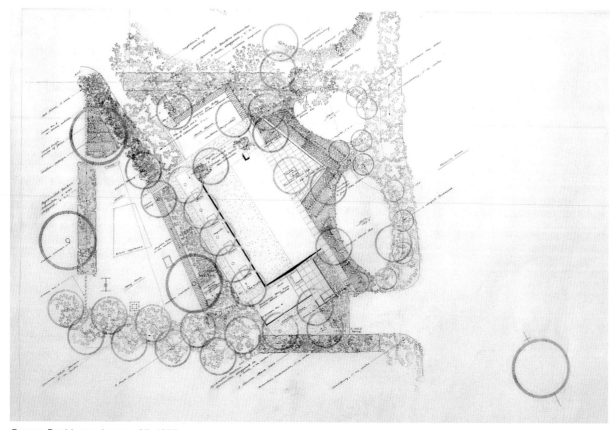

Rogers Residence January 25, 1955

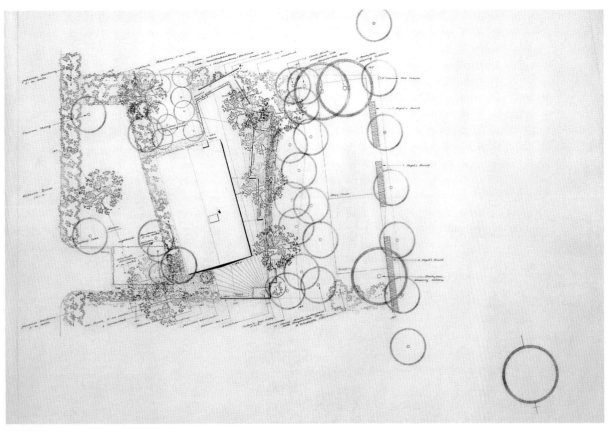

Blooston Residence February 10, 1955

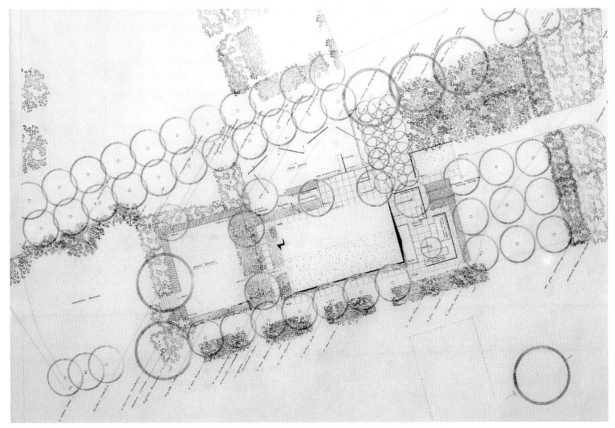

Buffmire Residence February 7, 1955

frequently as progressive or socialist—
was the provision of shared space across
property lines. The plan for David P. Coffin
illustrated here was an example; note the
proposed vegetable garden to the north,
intended as a complete rectangular figure
by inclusion of the adjoining owners' plot,
along with the semi-circular arrangement
of Apple trees and ground cover that
spans both properties. Elsewhere,
hedges and groves crossed boundaries
in the spirit of common interests.

Kiley's proposals relied on a simple
but delicate method of working in plan.
By using both meticulous pencil line work
and custom-made ink stamps with precise tonal and textural effects, each drawing conveyed the multiple layers of
ground plane, understory, and upper
canopy vegetation that were by now practiced and routine for Kiley and his staff.
Although no three-dimensional sketches
survive, the plans indicate a careful sense
of detail and craft; on the whole, they
contain a rich vocabulary of planted forms
and spatial improvisations that undoubtedly influenced Kiley's work for Irwin and
Xenia Miller in Columbus.

Segmented boundary hedges,
dense groves, trees in rows or grids,
and overlapping masses of ordered
vegetation link these projects formally
and spatially to Kiley's ideas in the
Miller Garden. In his proposal for the
Buffmire property, Kiley is most resolute in setting up a series of ordered
spaces that are proportionally affiliated
with the house and always orthogonal
to it. Here, the spatial resemblance
to the Miller Garden is instructive.
Although the two are worlds apart in
land area, resources, the role of the
architect and client, and overall intensity
of design effort, they both participate
in Kiley's pursuit of modern ways of
living and the development of modern
landscape space.

The Honeylocust allée one year after planting.

The Miller Garden: Icon of Modernism

Dan Kiley, whose six decades of practice in landscape architecture have produced a body of work of unequaled beauty and significance, has frequently described the Miller Garden as his first really modern project. That is a conspicuous and somewhat ambiguous utterance—the kind Kiley is known for. What does he mean by this? While his words underestimate the project's roots in the rebellious mood of his itinerant Harvard days and the edgy leanings of his early practice, and while they don't indicate what it means to be modern, it is nonetheless true that the Miller Garden has currency in any discussion of modernism in American landscape architecture. We should want to know: What makes the Miller Garden modern? Why has it come to be an icon?

Designers and followers of landscape architecture know the Miller Garden, but they have rarely examined it. Its status as an icon of modernism in America, like that of so many monuments of our modern culture, has come about more by a proliferation of images than by first-hand experience. Visits to the project are limited to protect the privacy of Irwin and Xenia Miller, who still occupy the house—and care for it with curatorial devotion—more than forty years after its construction. Because they managed to keep it largely from view, the garden was virtually unknown during the first 25 years after its completion. At a point in the early 1980s, after several discreet publications in which the garden's particulars were not fully disclosed, the Miller Garden emerged, an already mature landscape. This happened during a time of commotion and change, when scholars and designers began to mount a critical evaluation of their own intellectual traditions and attempted to define modernity within their discipline—indeed, it took the uncertainty and intellectual upheaval of postmodernism to finally give shape and purpose to modernism in landscape architecture. In the process, through images and brief descriptions, the Miller Garden became a touchstone.

Alan Ward's images of the Miller Garden have been studiously absorbed by designers of several generations—designers who have been drawn to the spatial qualities of the garden and house, rendered with pictorial grace in the photographs.

They have appeared in numerous publications.[1] Like architecture's archetypal modern projects, such as Le Corbusier's Villa Savoye in Poissy of 1929 or Mies van der Rohe's German National Pavilion at the International Exposition of 1929 in Barcelona, the Miller Garden is frequently cited. But unlike the regular flow of descriptive, interpretive, and theoretical literature about these pivotal architectural works, we've had no industry of critical examination and little in the way of debate on the substance of the built work itself. The images, it seems, have satisfied.

It is more than deserving of examination, and Kiley's claim for its modernity is worth probing for clues to the garden's stature. We must assume that when Kiley says the Miller Garden is "modern" that he means it carries some of the marks of modernism in both architecture and landscape architecture. From his earliest days as a student and practitioner, Kiley has sought a fusion of ideas that cross boundaries between architecture and landscape. He professes a rare kind of devotion to the space of nature and the constructed landscape, and an equal passion for the spatial possibilities in modern building. He was never bound by the limits of his field. He was drawn to those aspects of landscape architecture's history that were common with architecture, but also to its roots in the practical ordering of agricultural landscapes, in the botanical sciences, and in the arts. Like modernists in other fields such as architecture, literature, painting, or music, Kiley operated in an ever-widening culture, tending to shake loose from disciplinary traditions by applying new motivations, always seeking new transformations of process, material, and form.

Modernism in architecture was characterized by conscious and polemical breaks with its conventional meanings, pushed forward by technological change, the advantages of mass production, the emergence of new forms of industrial and corporate organization, and the vast development needs of modernizing populations. Because these forces altered not only the social purpose but also the essential codes of material expression in architecture, new forms of expression dominated all scales of building, including houses. Indeed, inasmuch as it condenses many of architecture's essential problems and motivations, the single detached house became a primary vehicle for the articulation of a modern architecture. The same cultural forces shaped the modern landscape, also; but the impacts of technology and mass production were evidenced more clearly at the scales of infrastructure and planning. In the garden they were more elusive, and responses to them more erratic. Modernism's impacts on the larger landscape were evident in the complex phenomenon of suburban expansion, and with the ever more ambitious harnessing of land resources and the infrastructure required to deliver them—think of the great impacts on landscape caused by the work of the Tennessee Valley Authority, the National Parks, or the building of parkways and highways. Most pervasively, landscape architects struggled with the accommodation of the automobile in every facet of American life. And while these forces changed our landscape in irreversible ways, landscape architecture's most primary entity—the garden—could and often did resist these forces. Kiley's work was one of the exceptions.

Polemical outbursts and declarations of modernist doctrine have been plentiful and are well documented in architecture; in landscape architecture, they have been neither routine nor vociferous. Kiley himself was one of the few who, with his fellow Harvard students Garrett Eckbo and James Rose, attempted to appropriate architecture's strident discourse in the late 1930s for the landscape, publishing a series of now well-known papers that challenged contemporary thinking at the scales of the site, city, and region.[2] They sought to reposition the garden: rather than accept its historical conventions and its role as a luxury for society, they argued for the garden as a metaphor, as society's essential place of inhabitation. They saw the garden as an armature that could shape design at all scales. But their argument for a focus on the problems of urbanism and settlement was the one most clearly heard. Ironically, the somewhat urgent and polemical tone they put forth promoted a spirited relevance for the garden in a new modernist discourse—but effectively buried it in practice. In time, the garden receded from view.[3] Because the material aspects of the garden—fundamentally plants and planted forms—were not to be discarded entirely for new substitutes, the works of modernism changed not what they were, but how they were employed. This implied transformations of formal language, not wholesale breaks or shifts. There were plenty of experiments. Kiley, Eckbo, Rose, and others produced many gardens that attempted to forge a modern garden language. But no die was cast. Because modernists also held that every site requires a specific response, gardens could not replicate architecture's reliance on iterative structural and expressive problems. There was no universal garden technology, no new production standard or requisite material change. So for Kiley, the search for a modern landscape was a spatial search: a drive to find space that did not depend on accepted pictorial conventions, or an old-world reliance on strict or complete enclosure and separation, or the replication of time-honored patterns and shapes, or the imitation of naturally occurring plant communities. He pursued this search through a medium that was traditional, but he found ways to make it dynamic and timeless.

As a modernist, Kiley himself demonstrates a kind of self-conscious balance among the forces of continuity and renewal. In conversation, he pays enormous tribute to his first employer, the great landscape architect Warren Manning, who taught him the most essential lessons of practice and instilled his love for the expressive potential of plants.[4] Fundamentally, Kiley sees himself as Manning's heir, and in this, he links himself to a generation of landscape professionals who defined the field's professional beginnings in America, including Charles Eliot, John C. Olmsted, and Frederick Law Olmsted, Sr. (for whom Manning had been chief plantsman for years), and to talented and sophisticated garden designers such as Beatrix Farrand and Harold Hill Blossom. On the other hand, Kiley identifies strongly with Fletcher Steele, who challenged the comfortable and aristocratic landscape orthodoxy in the 1920s and '30s by introducing European modernism to his countrymen. At Harvard, in the late 1930s, Kiley and his compatriots favored the ambitious new functional and spatial ideals of Walter Gropius over the mannered garden conventions of their own teachers. And after Harvard, Kiley associated with the leading modernist architects more than any landscape architect of his day, or even of his succeeding generation. All told, Kiley possessed over the course of his career the equanimity and self-assuredness needed to bridge between the useful traditional roots of practice and the necessary challenges to its very foundations.

Other clues to Kiley's modernity reside in his unusual professional stature and his long and productive relationship with his counterpart on the Miller project, Eero Saarinen. Notable among the defining characteristics of Kiley's public and professional image are his wry independence from the burdens of his field and his widely known conviction that design and life are inseparable. Saarinen mirrored this view. Eero was born into a highly cultivated design world and never parted from it. His life-long architectural ambitions were nearly pre-ordained: informed by the large-scale industrial building efforts in his father's studio, he eventually perfected the corporate architectural enterprise required to produce several major buildings at the same time. Yet equally important, he drew on his Scandinavian traditions and his parents' love of building, their devotion to craft and local practices of making, and their respect for traditional forms as a basis of knowledge and repository of cultural meaning. Who in this period could have evolved such a trusting, reciprocal relationship with Saarinen other than Dan Kiley?

This man was different from most landscape architects. He mistrusted the habits and conventions of his own profession, for a while fashioning a hybrid practice designing houses and landscape together. Eventually, he stopped making buildings, although his pursuits in architecture undoubtedly shaped his enduring commitment to abstraction and functional clarity. Early in his career, Kiley turned his disdain for what he perceived as an outdated, falsely aristocratic resistance to modernity among his landscape architecture peers into a highly modern life for himself and his family in rural New England: a deliberate separation from the city (not a suburban semi-detachment); a reliance on long distance motoring and air travel before either was fashionable or comfortable, so that he could pursue commissions across the nation; and a rather decentralized family life among several

dwellings and pavilions dispersed on a large tract of Vermont woodland, which enabled a workaholic life without the complete abandonment of familial responsibility. In Charlotte, life and work intersected deeply; and from all this, an unusually calm and robustly confident designer attracted staff and partners and collaborators and clients to come to this remote place in legendary proportions. This must have appealed immensely to an architect such as Eero Saarinen and to other modern thinkers as well, including Irwin and Xenia Miller. Go to Charlotte today, and you inevitably sense the completeness and serenity of life that enables Kiley to sustain his practice and his search and creates desire in others to be near it. Ask anyone who has spent time there; the reaction is nearly universal.

Both of these designers shared another characteristic sometimes thought absent in dedicated modernists. Again, both shaped their work with an unerring sense of modernity's impacts on life and space. But counter to the prevailing accusations of historical amnesia for the period, neither Saarinen nor Kiley worked in denial of the precedents that could be adapted for modern living. Devout modernist that he is, Kiley tells that he did not make a conscious reference to precedent, and one is inclined to believe him; but his knowledge of and respect for traditional uses of plants surely shaped his work at the Miller Garden. Kiley says of Saarinen that he did not make explicit use of precedents either, but he allows that Saarinen's limitless and passionate knowledge of architectural history was never far from the deliberations over technology and form. His regularly ordered structural system for the Miller House has traces of the central planning and multi-directional ordering of classical or renaissance pavilions, translated into a modernist sensibility in ways that Saarinen had observed in the buildings of Mies van der Rohe at Chicago's IIT; and it pursues a refinement of the structural expression that he had sought in several earlier projects—this in a period too frequently described as being without respect for precedent or history. Kiley, too, often identified as one of the rebels who rejected history, never did so. Rather, he rejected the pompous intellectual authority and tired formal manners of his teachers and the elite of his profession.

Moreover, while he loved the plants and planted forms that were commonplace conventions in his field, he refused to accept that there were rules for their use. He wanted a modern sensibility, especially toward the simple organization of space for function and for visual beauty. Both love of nature and a discerning respect for history enabled this sensibility.

Kiley's claim for the Miller Garden's modernity is a confident self-appraisal: here, he realized a consummate joining of mutual aims between Saarinen and himself. Here, both designers were engaged in the pursuit of transparency, that modernist desire of seeing and experiencing seamlessly across the boundaries between architecture and landscape. They also sought a focus on functional clarity as a means of expression; an interest in a rational ordering of space; and overall, an unrelenting search for modern ways of living. Moreover, if these were ongoing pursuits for both, it may be said that in the Miller project, they were pushed by Saarinen for nearly three years of development on the project, resulting in a refined, perhaps overwrought house. But for Kiley, the achievement of an extraordinary level of abstraction and invention was realized in his most open and unencumbered site up to that time. The flatness of the land and the relative absence of physical constraints set up an open field where he could act out his increasing ambitions for a modern spatial clarity. Here the syntax of spatial definition that had been building on smaller residential projects and larger institutional works was enabled as never before. Kiley's earlier projects had frequently relied on angular geometries, self-conscious shapes, and visually charged spatial overlaps—as if in reaction to the more stable and resolved devices of previous generations. At the Miller Garden, in the context of a regular, nearly flat site and a rational building plan, those charged geometries were released from his repertoire, and another kind of spatial attitude took over. The result was more elegant than a mere residence, more finely ordered than a corporate setting, as abstract as any art institution, and as serene as any sacred space.

Reciprocal Aims: Transparency in Building and Landscape

Mies van der Rohe's Farnsworth House

Concerns for lightness, transparency, clarity of structural expression, and continuity between inside and outside were part of the agenda of modernism in architecture, and they were certainly paramount for Eero Saarinen in the years leading up to the Miller project. Especially during the late 1940s and early '50s, Saarinen pursued what the historian and critic Peter Papademetriou has called a "questioning modernism"—a rigorous research on the tectonics, means of production, and resulting expression in new kinds of industrial buildings and public spaces.[5] Such an inquiry was evident in Saarinen's work on an unbuilt residential commission known as California Case Study House No. 8 of the early 1940s, with the brilliant young designer Charles Eames, and in his project for the General Motors Technical Center in Bloomfield Hills, Michigan, begun in 1945 and realized exactly during the years of the Miller project.[6] In both of these projects, through concerns that could be described as both technical and humanist, Saarinen's push for clarity and economy of structure gave primacy to thin steel and large expanses of glass. Transparency reigned. And in these years, the god of transparency for Saarinen was Mies van der Rohe.[7]

By the 1950s, the German master architect Ludwig Mies van der Rohe, practicing first in Weimar Germany and after 1938 in Chicago, had pursued the relations among space, structure, and transparency in all manner of building types, from the aggressively asymmetrical German Pavilion at Barcelona in 1929 to the sublimely classical buildings for the Illinois Institute of Technology from 1939–56. At the domestic scale, it was the house for Dr. Edith Farnsworth of 1946–50 in Plano, Illinois, that emerged as the signal domestic investigation of transparency, the quest for a light-filled box as the perfect device for residing in the landscape. Mies's own often-quoted description of transparency's importance was poetic and clear: "If you view nature through the glass walls of the Farnsworth House it gains a more profound significance than if viewed from outside. More of nature is expressed—nature becomes part of a larger totality."[8] Elevated over the ground on a raised podium, the structure of the house was as thin and light

as possible, and the enclosed prismatic volume was simply wrapped in plate glass—in Mies's words, *beinahe nichts*—"almost nothing." This was the conceptually clear paradigm of transparency for architects. But for Kiley, a transparent connection between building and site meant something more.

At the Farnsworth House, Mies depended on a traditional conception of landscape as framed and objectified and remote, as a scene to behold from a fixed place of observation. One of Eero Saarinen's first proposals to the Millers, a raised platform house situated close to the Flatrock River and within the limits of the floodplain, had similarities to the Farnsworth House too obvious to deny. But when Saarinen's proposal for the Millers implied a similar reduction of the landscape to background, the astute Irwin Miller recognized it for what it was: an uninhabited scene, a rhetorical conceit that limited opportunities for leisure, recreation, cultivation, and functional subdivision. It was the opposite of the modern landscape for living. A shimmering vessel akin to the Farnsworth House demanded a restrained, almost untouched—Mies would say natural—landscape. The Millers wanted more. Eventually, Saarinen was able to reconcile their needs for privacy, livability, and separation of use with the desire for openness and transparency in a house that rested firmly on its site. And Dan Kiley answered the need for spatial continuity and livability not with untended nature, but rather with a garden of enormous artifice.

Entrance, Barcelona Pavilion

Independence of column, wall, and roof, Barcelona Pavilion

Although the radically clear ideal of the Farnsworth House lost countenance with both house and garden in Columbus, there are common motivations in the project that can be more strongly related to the influence of Mies: the unfolding and irregular contour of continuous space, inside and outside, that we can see in the Barcelona Pavilion; counterbalanced with this, a tendency toward classical planning and studied, delicate proportion, as illustrated most notably in Mies's long span pavilions at Stuttgart in the 1920s and at Chicago's IIT; and the manipulation of the clear order and quasi-regulated freedom inherent in the modernist grid, inside and out.[9] Dan Kiley has generally affirmed these associations; Kevin Roche, Saarinen's assistant on the project and eventual inheritor of the firm's legacy, has ascribed them to Mies.[10]

Kiley's design strategies converge with those of Eero Saarinen in potent ways. Throughout the project, Kiley employs an overriding spatial logic with substantial variation, something like a set of simple rules with allowable interruptions. Like Saarinen, he engages only in right-angled relations, but gives emphasis to subtle shifts and asymmetries; he likewise pursues a simple functional zoning of spaces, exposing some adjacencies but hiding others away, without worrying about frontality or decorum in the traditional sense. He uses what must be understood as very ordinary spatial conventions (allée, enclosing hedge, grove, meadow, and overlook)—but he never depends on conventional rules.

Yet where Saarinen's plan is sharply contained by its careful dimensions and insistent order, the garden gains luxury and freedom in all these devices.

Consider the relation between structure and space in the house. Comparison to the Barcelona Pavilion is instructive. Saarinen's Miller House has an enormous roof—120 by 101 feet—held in place by a structural steel grid supported on sixteen cruciform columns. In the Barcelona Pavilion, we also have cruciform columns and what appear to be load-bearing walls; but the relationships among wall and column and ceiling are visually complex. At times the walls appear to support the roof—but often not; the walls are extremely thin, and the roof glides past them. Upon closer inspection, the roof appears to rest on the column's polished chrome flange (although it actually pierces through the plaster). The visual result is that the roof plane soars, uninterrupted, as a surface overhead, almost free of the walls. Roof, walls, columns, and floor are seen as independent elements shaping a dynamic volume. This ensures a variable and indeterminate spatial continuity in the Barcelona project. Indeed, it challenges basic conceptions of building and landscape, compelling us to question what is inside, what is outside. Transparency here is defined as a desire for unclear boundaries, for spatial ambiguity. The pavilion is sometimes a building, sometimes a garden.[11]

Now look at the Miller House: the expression of the column's connection with the roof structure is different. Column and roof are joined in an obvious load-and-

28

Structure and enclosure, Miller House

Podium, Miller House

support structural connection—rigid, fixed, and symmetrically uniform. The wall, with its panelized veneer construction and its frequent interruptions of glass and void, never appears to hold up the roof; the column clearly does. Put simply, columns support, walls divide. What is inside is inside; what is outside is also clear. Perhaps for Saarinen this was more intellectually honest, and more visibly structural; it satisfies something Mies had sought in a different matter, an "unambiguous constructive appearance" of structure.[12] Rather than exploit a complex physical overlapping of inside and outside, as Mies had at Barcelona, Saarinen's Miller House is structurally resolute and unambiguous. Consequently, it was Kiley who could more vigorously pursue overlap and transparency through other devices, in the manipulation of the space immediately outside the walls of the house.

Other moments of sophistication in the house appealed to Kiley. With such a big roof and a deep cross-section, the need for daylight inside required that the roof be perforated in some way. The corrective measure was something of an invention for Saarinen: a convergence between structure and light, where the welded structural chassis of column and roof became the principal source of daylight in the depths of the house. The grid is really a channel, 2'-6" in width, that contains a horizontal glazed diffuser and peaked glass housing above. The channel admits ambient light by day; and it has a fluorescent tube and occasional spots so that it also emits light at night, throughout the column grid. It is

the light of this channel, day and night, that reveals the relation between overall order and alteration that Kiley would later exploit: at times, the building envelope is inches from the channel and raked in light; at other times, the wall retreats inbound from the grid and the light diffuses. The same happens inside. When the living space opens up in the middle, the light grid spans across the space, always registering position with respect to the structural logic.

Channeled light and reflected light also underscore the tectonics of the exterior walls and glazing. The soffit and the structural steel frame are painted bright white; you can detect shadow and subtle reflection in these surfaces. The podium, which extends one 2'-6" module beyond the line of the soffit overhang, was cast in white terrazzo at Kiley's suggestion.[13] This allows the reflected light off the glazed panels to brighten the adjacent terrazzo and thus reveal the pattern of alternating glazing and slate enclosure from the view along the side of the house. The lovely dark Alabama marble, some five feet wide by almost nine feet high, is proportionally massive, but it is plainly articulated here as a delicately thin skin; its role as enclosure—not structure—is clear, and its textured surface is sensuously depicted by the light. We sense not the heaviness of a natural sedimented stone, but rather its lightness, and we think of the precision and delicacy of a careful splitting operation that brings forth the stone's interior structure in such a thin veneer.

Functionalism and Spatial Freedom

It was Kiley's influence on the space immediately adjacent to the building envelope that made for greater transparency between inside and outside. Saarinen's proposed twenty-five-foot podium typified the modernist conception of the ground plane as a uniform, equivalent surface marked by a grid and bounded by a clear edge—by definition, a demarcation between the built world and the natural world. But this kind of abstract dualism, one that proposes a distinction between human culture and the natural world, was anathema to Kiley. Rather than accept the simplistic man/nature separation, he has always insisted that "man *is* nature." Here, he could actualize his belief. By reducing the twenty-five foot terrazzo area to ten feet, measuring just two-and-a-half feet beyond the roof overhang, Kiley defined the podium more as a continuation of the floor inside, less a taut planar architectural field. Around the podium, he planted a slightly raised bed of ivy, along with paired Magnolias on two of the sides and paired European Weeping Beeches on the opposite sides. In maturity, these trees envelop the house, making its exceptionally long proportions—really institutional in scale—satisfyingly domestic. Instead of a uniform abstraction of the ground plane, the ground cover and trees provide a supple, spatial field, characterized by shade and shadow, mass and void, and alternation of enclosure and view. Kiley's was a richer conception, more varied if less abstract, certainly more vivid in experience. Transparency and spatial continuity were achieved not just by extension of the floor surface, but by the close presence of ground cover, trunk, leaf, branch, and canopy. In this case it came not from a radical modern spatial invention, but rather from a nearly instinctual and practiced attitude toward the grounding of building and site.

The functional and spatial organization of the interior spaces of the house also informed Kiley's planning of the garden. Saarinen organized the principal rooms in the house into four main blocks that allowed for some privacy or separation, and allowed the most "public" program in the house to take up the open middle zone. Each of the four partitioned groups, including the parents' quarters, the children's rooms, the carport, household help and guest quarters, and the kitchen wing, is treated as a separate volume. These are held to the corners and directionally rotated, yielding an asymmetry that would be more forceful were it not confined by the hovering roof above. The balance of interior space, the shared overlap between enclosed volumes, provides for living space, dining, and sitting space. There is something serenely 1950s-modern in this space, and there is a distinct lack of conventional hierarchy and frontality. There is no front or back; instead, four facades confront four directions, in true pavilion fashion.

When it came to accommodating the program of spaces that surround the house, Kiley built on Saarinen's functionalist approach. Kiley considers functional relationships as a pragmatic foundation of design, even though he also admits that people often misunderstand the importance of use in determining form and placement. Function, he says, is a word many designers don't like.[14] At the Miller project, he allowed a logic of functional convenience to supersede the polite hierarchy of spaces that neighboring homes displayed. Rather than discreetly hiding the usually private spaces away from the street, he placed the greenhouse (which became a guest house), vegetable gardens, and tennis courts (never built) on the street side of the house, and shifted the more passive and less defined recreations further inbound. The swimming pool, planned in the original scheme but completed during the 1970s, was placed at the edge of the property, adjacent to the drive—but properly screened for privacy from the neighbors and from the house with the enclosing hedge.

The proportions of these spaces are generous, and in the four and one-half acres of the upper plateau, the overlaps among adjacent spaces seem carefully

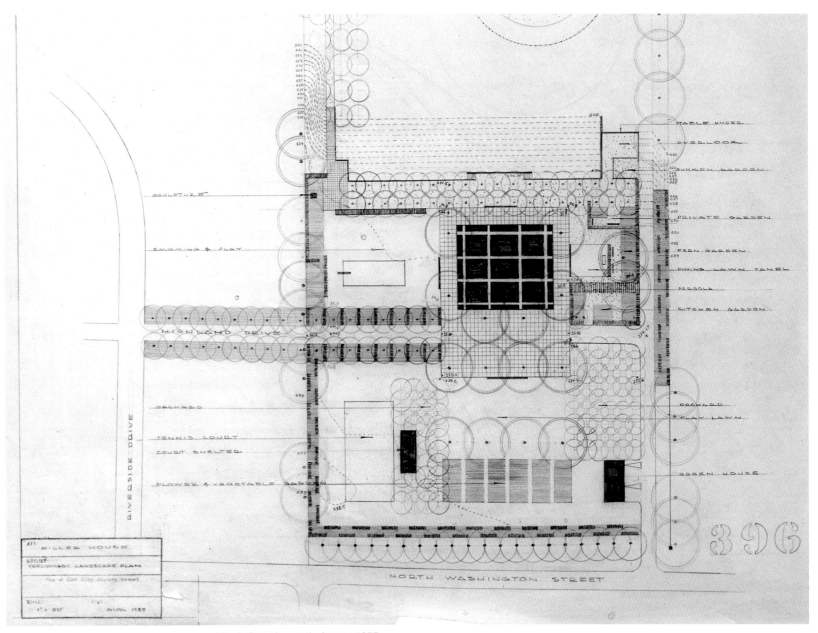

*Kiley's first plan, early August 1955.
The garden spaces of the upper plateau
changed little after this first complete
sketch. Note that Kiley represented the
house plan by indicating the structural
grid as a light channel.*

controlled yet relaxed. The sophistication of layout matches Saarinen's interior organization. In the house, there is an overall structural order, modified by placing partitions and rooms on or off the grid and rotating the orientation of spaces around a center. Kiley does this too, but in more open-ended ways. Kiley's overall device for organizing the upper plateau is a crisp and very nearly square 450-foot frame, which, as several critics have noted, has a sub-organizing tendency approximating nine-square division. But not exactly. Its subdivision is somewhat regular, but it is irregularly presenced. Some spaces, including the drying yard, the parking court, and the swimming pool area, are defined by the enclosing hedge, in staggered parallel or perpendicular alignment; others, including the orchards, are without immediate boundary. Kiley's orthogonal order is really more a register, a constant and variable field in which only right-angled relations are allowed. Indeed, it is easy to see how both house and site resist anything but right angles. Yet it is not a grid, nor is it an even subdivision of squares. It's a kind of guiding compass, the kind Midwestern farmers had inherited from the national grid and had applied as a device to order their fields, hedges, farm compounds, and rows of corn and wheat. A natural tendency for the straight and orderly, adjusted for circumstance when necessary, but dependably quadrilateral. In Kiley's sure hands, it need be no more than that.

Typically Kiley did not prefer to accept site-planning decisions made before his arrival, but he trusted Saarinen. Fortunately, Saarinen and the Millers had agreed on siting the house at the front edge of a plateau that separated the floodplain from dry land. Here the house afforded a westerly view over the lower meadow toward the Flatrock River, and it allowed Saarinen the modernist pleasure of exploiting the site's strong horizontality. But while Saarinen was satisfied conceptually with horizon and distance, these were only points of departure for Kiley. From here, he could pursue the subtleties of orientation, variations in exposure to sun and wind, the orchestration of view, the organization of outdoor rooms related to the house, the shaping of the edge of the plateau and the slope to the meadow. The end result, especially after the maturation of Kiley's plantations on the upper plateau and the

Perpendicular segments of the enclosing Arborvitae hedge

allée, is that the house sits calmly, almost classically, on the river's natural levee. There it has a graceful, protected repose, and it commands a stunning view across the low open meadow toward the river.

The flatness of this upper portion of the site was one of the keys to Kiley's freedom. The plateau, which exhibits a richer upland soil condition than those of the slope and the meadow area, was nearly dead level—less than two feet of elevation change in more than 400 feet—and nearly devoid of tree cover, save a few trees along the property boundary. Think of this flat plane, regularly sided and uninterrupted, and you realize Kiley's unencumbered freedom to determine the subdividing proportions and relations. There is no circumstantial oddity, no accident of previous existence, no trace of prior occupation to fit things to. That is so unusual in landscape, where there is always something there before you start. All of the relations within the orthogonal register are negotiable, not conditioned by bumps or shapes on the ground. How paradigmatic: the modern space, without the usual contingency of place. Kiley had the freedom to place each separate garden event— each form—almost as he wished. He was comfortable with such freedom. "I feel that one should start on a problem with a *tabula rasa*, a clean slate," he has said; at the Miller Garden, more than anywhere previously, he discovered beauty in the absence of constraint.[15] It was the modernist's ideal, a freedom to exploit the devices of spatial order.

Freedom led to invention. Consider the Arborvitae hedge that forms the enclosing frame of the plateau, so admired by designers since its publication in the 1980s. Staggered hedges were not unheard of in the planting schemes of earlier generations, and they had appeared in Kiley's previous residential work with surprising variation. But this one is more complex. It begins as a staggered pattern with a density and thickness hedges don't ordinarily have. In its doubled and staggered nature, its alignment can be easily modified, more so than the traditional single-line hedge. Gaps in the hedge are not seen as interruptions, because the gap is an essential characteristic. And there is always slight tension in the overlapping segments of both perpendicular and parallel arrangements. In the oblique view and even straight on, the soft texture of Arborvitae reflects a highlight, suggesting depth; in combination with the adjacent shadow, we understand the hedge not just as a boundary, but as a thickened, active, surrounding shape. Kiley adjusts it or loses it altogether where leakage is possible or desired, where existing pines make closure unnecessary.

The most beautiful manifestation of the hedge at the entrance drive has become a legend of its own. Here the so-called baffle hedge, a series of parallel hyphens of pyramidal Arborvitae alternating with Horsechestnut trees, acted in sequence as a series of scrims, allowing only gradual disclosure of the house and grounds upon arrival. This kind of hedge would have been familiar to garden makers of sixteenth-century Italy as a stage device in the garden theater; Kiley used it to comparable effect but made it seem refreshingly modern. Unfortunately, the Arborvitae hedge would not survive the eventual shade of the Horsechestnut trees, so this scheme was replaced in 1973 with a low continuous taxus hedge. Finally, toward the meadow, the framing hedge is replaced altogether by the allée, which gives way to light and openness. In all this, the hedge as a frame is systematic, inventive, and highly alterable—and following no particular rules of convention or measure, save its constant ten foot height.

The garden spaces within the hedge enclosures—the "adult garden," the Apple orchards, the oak trees and lawns, the swimming pool area, and the allée—all behave within the orthogonal register, but there is always a twist that saves them from being overly conventional or prosaic. In the orchard of apple trees, which came from the Millers' own farm outside Columbus, Kiley applies the standard equivalent spacing of trees but leaves a void in the center. The result is that we see the backlighted trunks in silhouette, and the rectangular shape of the entire plantation is registered with a central blast of light. Suddenly the orchard is more than a grid; we sense a horizon of space moving through it, coming to rest momentarily in the center. At that point, it is both orchard and garden, evoking the image of cultivation and uniquely establishing a place we can occupy.

In the original "adult garden," which was modified when Kiley's Redbuds became overmature and needed to be removed, spatial definition was complex and dynamic and rather free. Along with two gridded clusters of Redbud, single hedges of Ilex were employed as a series of perpendicular lines, with gaps at the intersecting points. This simple device produced enclosure, but without actual closure, allowing the space to be defined but also to escape across and beyond the Redbud grove. The overlap carried a sense of extension and anticipation. Compositionally, it borrowed on the kind of abstraction and visual tension we have seen in the obscured boundaries of space in Mies's Barcelona Pavilion. The pinwheeling, as Kiley calls it, had been pursued in Saarinen's house with modest success; but Kiley knew its potential in the landscape from previous experiments on smaller residential projects. Here he applied it with confidence. It is unfortunate that the Ilex hedges were removed and the Redbuds were replaced with Crabapples. They are lovely enough, but are heavier and coarser in habit, depending more on a showy display of color and foliage than on the dappled light and elegant upright trunks of Redbuds. This alteration of the fabric of Kiley's careful spatial handiwork was perhaps the only notable departure from an otherwise faithful protectorship of the property.

Upsetting Convention: The Honeylocust Allée

Kiley's most inventive use of conventional garden form, and perhaps the moment in the garden that has been most influential on recent generations of designers, is in the allée at the meadow-edge of the plateau. Thirty-six Moraine Honeylocusts, with a light canopy and graceful branching, form a linear space that seems almost wedged in across the entire western edge of the plateau, above the carefully graded slope that leads to the meadow below. Although traditionally such double rows of trees are intended to direct space axially, as movement space, here no axis exists. Axis implies a centerline of reference — usually, but not always, of a symmetrical kind. Usually, an axis originates in, or aligns with, a structure of spatial significance; here, the allée is not dependent on objects or on architecture. It glides sidelong past the house. Kiley's allée cannot be axial; it just begins and ends hard on fixed vertical surfaces, both punctuated by platforms and sculpture — but neither end of which could be said to generate a true axis of extension.

Although published images of the allée often focus on the reclining figure by Henry Moore at the northern terminus, the Moore sculpture was added later, and it is frankly peripheral to Kiley's intent. Here we have an invention: the creation of an expanding view laterally across an allée, rather than the traditional view down its linear path. Kiley has said the allée began with function — giving shade and definition to the long edge of the house — and he has likened this treatment to the Renaissance architect Pirro Ligorio's long balustraded strolling terrace at the Villa D'Este in Tivoli, situated high above the fantastic water garden and perched for dramatic views toward Rome.[16] The comparison makes sense. But as an allée, Kiley's space gains in complexity. At the Miller Garden, the allée's measured cadence and its topographic relations — high and level on one side, dropping away on the other — make it a superb strolling space, but that is not its principal role. Our most usual experience of it is on the oblique, looking from the house and its podium across to the meadow. Less a processional space and more a loggia, it defined a distinct orientation toward the west for Saarinen's

The allée, more loggia than axis

multi-directional pavilion. A westward view was symbolically rich and spatially right for the site. As the slope drops away, the bright westward exposure of the meadow dominates; the horizon and the sky draw the more forceful visual focus across the allée. This was so modern: the normally directional corridor of movement, now deployed as the oblique edge between the ordered spaces of the plateau and the great void of the flood plain. The carefully graded, entirely flat space of the allée is at once a commanding space of occupation and a preamble to the void beyond. Kiley's choice of a soft tan crushed stone surface, like the compacted earth of French bosquets and allées, always puts the trunks in clear register; because the canopy is high and light, we see every trunk in series, and the order is clear. The image is indelible, an absolutely recognizable signifier of modern space that has appeared on book jackets and magazine covers. It is an icon that has influenced space in residential, corporate, and public projects untold times. In a tour-de-force of truly modernist proportions, Kiley had transformed the conventional device of the axis and resurrected the ancient and beautiful space of trees in long, straight lines.

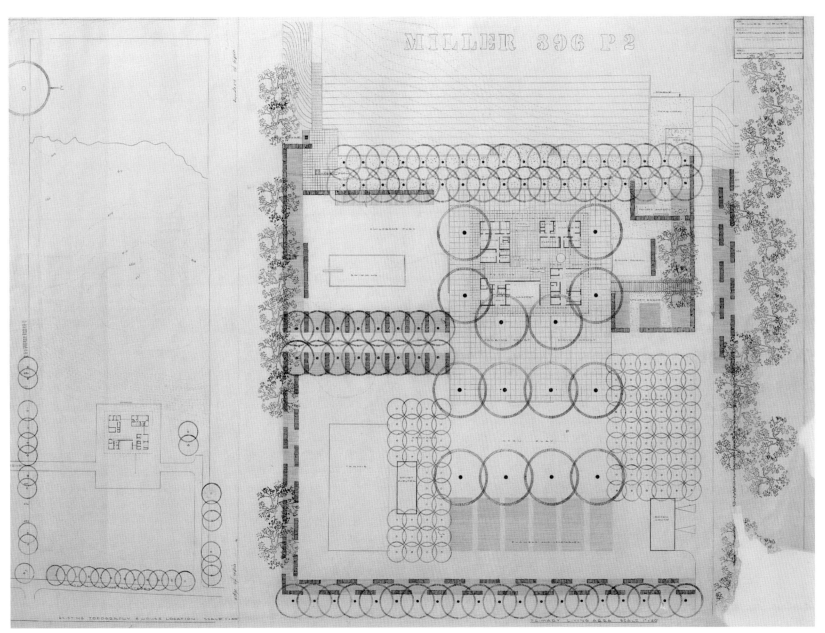

Kiley's second plan, late August 1955.
Here Kiley represented the organization
of rooms in the house, emphasizing a
comparable asymmetrical spatiality
between house and site.

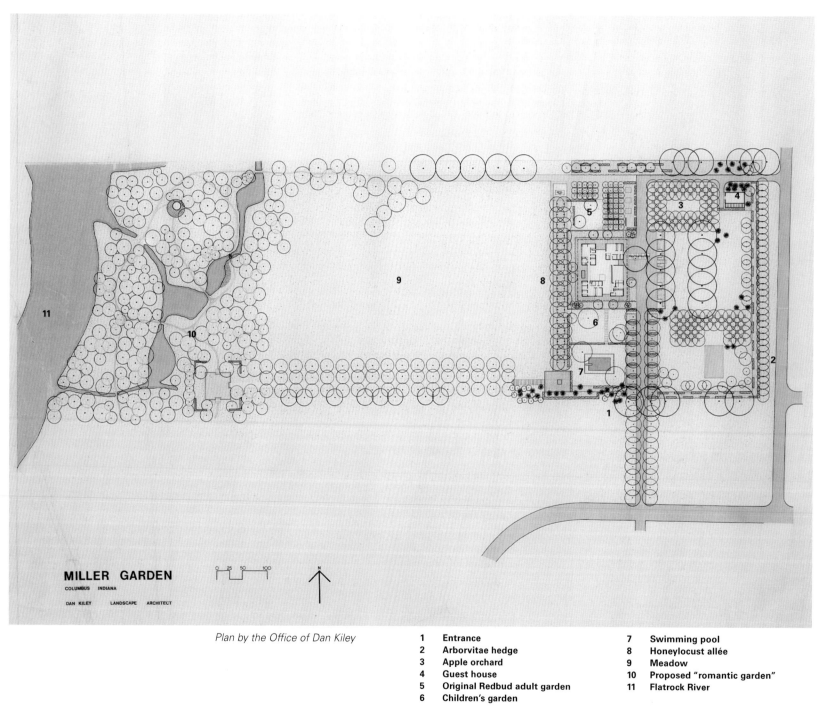

MILLER GARDEN

COLUMBUS INDIANA

DAN KILEY LANDSCAPE ARCHITECT

0 25 50 100

N

Plan by the Office of Dan Kiley

1	Entrance	7	Swimming pool
2	Arborvitae hedge	8	Honeylocust allée
3	Apple orchard	9	Meadow
4	Guest house	10	Proposed "romantic garden"
5	Original Redbud adult garden	11	Flatrock River
6	Children's garden		

Rediscovery

While Dan Kiley has thought the Miller Garden to be more the mark of modernity for his own body of work than for his profession at large, it deserves a wider claim: in landscape architecture's belated, deliberative search for its own modernity, the Miller Garden was there to fill the void as its most enduring icon. It was not always so. Perhaps we had never recognized such a garden as this one, without obvious figural geometries, or without curving lines and organic shapes, without the simplistic imitation of nature as irregular form. Nature here was ordered and spatially clear. This garden seemed so carefully conceived, so analytically derived. Appearing as it did during a period of nascent development of a new kind of landscape scholarship, and during a revival of landscape architecture's most ancient and noble form of expression—the garden—we were ready to understand Kiley's work, ready to appreciate it. A small but growing number of critics and historians were willing to make a case for it. Because it had remained little known for more than twenty years, it had by the time of its appearance reached a kind of maturity of growth and habit that made it instantly palpable and extraordinarily spatial, even in photographs. We loved those photographs. It was as if the garden had had no infancy—something our landscapes always struggle with. Its absolutely impeccable condition, fostered by a level of caring maintenance unmatched almost anywhere, assured us of a sense of the modern landscape as finely crafted artifice, and in this, we had a newly legitimizing claim for the field.

In the Miller Garden, Kiley found his modern space: imbued with transparency, and carefully balanced between tension and freedom. He achieved this through mutual purposes with a driven architect, and also through his own singular sense of the demands and pleasures of modern living. In Saarinen's house, we saw an intellectual and analytical space, a space so strenuously in pursuit of the most inspired tectonic craft of its time that it became not a great work of architecture but an elegant period piece. But in the garden, we see a timeless space, modern—but not fixed to a moment in the modernist chronology. Not one idea, not polemical, not totalizing, not even formally resolved—just intelligently and softly juxtaposed.

Once discovered—really *re*discovered—the careful order and calm spatial syntax of Kiley's work at the Miller Garden appealed to those who wished to have the garden return to the center of landscape architecture's domain. It had nearly disappeared, partly because of the polemics of Kiley's own generation and the imperative to pursue more pressing social agendas confronting American modernization and suburbanization. Those were important enterprises, undeniably. But unlike so many landscape architects who charged themselves with modernism's great challenges, Kiley never abandoned the garden. He always believed in it. And it was this, his most beautiful project, that restored our faith in designing domestic landscape space. Contrary to the image projected by a generation of scholars and landscape architects who were suspicious of modernism and who claimed it had destroyed traditions, Kiley did not reject the formal garden devices of enclosure, symmetry, and axis that he had inherited from earlier generations. Rather, he transformed them, reconciled them with a freedom and inventiveness that made them available again for exploitation. For a younger generation ready to acclaim both modernist and postmodern sensibilities in the garden, the open-ended geometries and spatial dissonances that we found customary by the mid-1980s were enabled by the discovery of the Miller Garden. Kiley's gentle upsetting of conventions ultimately loosed us of a dependence on resolved geometries and overtly mannered devices; and it also renewed our interest in the materials of landscape. In his hands, modern space became more than an abstraction of the series or the grid, more than an elaboration of pattern. In the process, the fundamental tools of garden design—planted forms and space—could again be valued for their rightful place in landscape architecture, as a medium of expression and spatial definition, with precise yet nearly infinite possibilities for meaning. It wasn't the Miller Garden alone that did this, to be sure. But there is no doubt that the Miller Garden's rediscovery helped us to rethink modernism as a condition that was at its best exploratory, inclusive, reflective and analytical, at times inventive, yet also critically engaged with history. For Kiley, it was a threshold in a modern career and in the search for modern space. For the rest of us, it is our icon.

Notes

A Place No One Knows

1 See "A Contemporary Palladian Villa" in *Architectural Forum* , September, 1958, 126–31. Also, "A New Concept of Beauty," *House & Garden*, February, 1959, 58–71. The next significant appearance of the Miller Garden was in *Built Landscapes: Gardens in the Northeast*, the catalogue for a 1984 exhibition at the Brattleboro Museum and Art Center curated by Michael Van Valkenburgh. Photographs were by Alan Ward.

2 *Architectural Record*, January, 1990, 67.

3 Interview with Irwin and Xenia Miller, September 24, 1996 in Columbus, Indiana.

4 Interview with Irwin and Xenia Miller, September 24, 1996 in Columbus, Indiana.

5 Interview with Kevin Roche, March 6, 1998.

6 All Kiley quotations are from interviews conducted by the author between November 1996 and August 1998.

7 The design is described in a January 24, 1963 letter from Kiley's associate, Douglas Sampson, to Xenia Miller.

The Miller Garden: Icon of Modernism

1 On the publication history of the Miller Garden, its reception, and its role in what I call the "return to the garden," see my essay, "Dan Kiley's Miller Garden: Coming to Light" in William Saunders, ed., *Daniel Urban Kiley: Early Gardens*, Princeton Architectural Press, 1999. Portions of that essay are excerpted here. Alan Ward's photographs appear in *Built Landscapes: Gardens in the Northeast*, Michael Van Valkenburgh, curator, Brattleboro, The Brattleboro Museum and Art Center, 1984; and in Alan Ward, *American Designed Landscapes: A Photographic Interpretation*, Washington D.C., Spacemaker Press, 1998; and elsewhere.

2 Garrett Eckbo, Daniel U. Kiley, James C. Rose, "Landscape Design in the Urban Environment", *The Architectural Record*, May, 1939; "Landscape Design in the Rural Environment", *The Architectural Record*, August, 1939; "Landscape Design in the Primeval Environment", *The Architectural Record*, February, 1940.

3 For re-published versions and critical discussion of the Eckbo-Kiley-Rose papers, see Marc Treib, *Modern Landscape Architecture: A Critical Review*, Cambridge: The MIT Press, 1993. Treib's book on the whole is proof that the Eckbo-Kiley-Rose writings of the 1930s had their greater effect not on practice in those years but on the past ten years of new scholarship on modernism. My claim that the garden receded from view is evidenced in the low position it held in professional publications and in design curricula from the 1940s through the 1980s. See my "Dan Kiley's Miller Garden: Coming to Light," op. cit. California must be noted as the great exception to this. For Garrett Eckbo's role in this, see also Treib and Dorothée Imbert, *Garrett Eckbo: Modern Landscapes for Living*, Berkeley: University of California Press, 1997.

4 Kiley's view of his place in a lineage of American landscape architects is often discussed in his informal lectures to students; these thoughts have also been repeated in conversations with the author, especially during September 1997 in Charlotte, Vermont.

5 Papademetriou, Peter. "Coming of Age: Eero Saarinen and Modern American Architecture," in *Perspecta: 21, Yale Architectural Journal*, New York: Yale University and Rizzoli International Publications, 1984. 116–43.

6 Ibid. 121, 131.

7 Kevin Roche, in conversation with David Dillon, Peter Papademetriou, and the author, noted that Saarinen was especially fascinated with Mies's work during these years. March 1998, North Haven, Connecticut.

8 Quoted in Fritz Neumeyer, "Space for Reflection: Block versus Pavilion," in Franz Schulz, ed., *Mies van der Rohe: Critical Essays*, New York, Museum of Modern Art, 1989. 169. Also quoted in Caroline Constant, "The Barcelona Pavilion as Landscape Garden: Modernity and the Picturesque," in *AA Files* No. 20, Autumn 1990. 46–54.

9 Gregg Bleam has made a convincing case for these themes. He describes the house as having a "pinwheel" organization of rooms around the periphery of a large rectangular structure; this rotational strategy yields a studiously unregulated and varied space at the center and the perimeter, and Bleam has appropriately suggested that Kiley built on this spatial device in arranging the spaces of the garden. Kiley confirms this reading. "Modern and Classical Themes in the Work of Dan Kiley," in Treib, *Modern Landscape Architecture*. 220–49.

10 Kiley in conversation, September 1997; Roche in conversation, March 1998.

11 Robin Evans discusses Saarinen's structural honesty and deceit in the Barcelona Pavilion in a brilliant essay, "Mies van der Rohe's Paradoxical Symmetries," in his *Translations from Drawing to Building and Other Essays*, Cambridge: The MIT Press, 1997.

12 Comay, Rebecca. "Almost Nothing: Heidegger and Mies," in *The Presence of Mies*, Detlef Mertens, ed., New York: Princeton Architectural Press, 1994. 179–189.

13 Kiley in conversation with the author, September 1997.

14 Ibid.

15 Kiley, in Warren T. Bird and Reuben Rainey, eds., *The Works of Dan Kiley: A Dialogue on Design Theory*, Proceedings of the 1st Annual Symposium on Landscape Architecture, University of Virginia, 1982. 34.

16 Ibid.

Alan Ward first photographed the Miller House for an architecture photography project in 1976. Two years later, he was commissioned to photograph the garden for the Harvard exhibition, "Dan Kiley: Classicist in the Modern Landscape." Those photographs were once again exhibited in another Harvard exhibition, "Built Landscapes: Gardens in the Northeast," in 1983. He returned to photograph the garden again in 1996 for his book, *American Designed Landscapes: A Photographic Interpretation.*

Street edge, enclosing Arborvitae hedge

Drive, after removal of baffle hedge

South lawn and hedge

Entry drive

*Remnant Honeylocusts from
the original allée planting*

Central space in the Apple orchard

Backlit trees in the Apple orchard

*Allée, ground cover, and European
Weeping Beech shape space at the
western edge of the house*

*Northern terminus of the allée from
the podium*

*View across the floodplain to the
walk at the edge of the meadow*

Ordered space in the Honeylocust allée

High, light canopy of the Honeylocust allée

Original Redbuds in the adult garden,
later replanted with Crabapples

*South lawn and approach to the
swimming pool area*

Alexander Girard's pool gate in the
enclosing hedge

*Swimming pool, enclosed by
Arborvitae hedge on four sides*

*Fine texture and imposing scale of
hedge enclosure*

Alexander Girard's gate spans the service drive

*The guest house is visible from below
the canopy of the orchard*

*The adult garden lawn captures
shadow and light*

Mature European Weeping Beeches
shade the space between inside
and outside